THE BOOK ABOUT
BOOKS

Chris Powling

Illustrated by Scoular Anderson

A & C Black • London

For
Sean O'Flynn
who found all this out for himself
C.P.

First published 2000 by
A & C Black (Publishers) Ltd
35 Bedford Row, London WC1R 4JH

ISBN 0-7136-5478-3

Text copyright © 2000 Chris Powling
Illustrations copyright © 2000 Scoular Anderson

A CIP catalogue record for this book is
available from the British Library.

Extract from 'Park in the Dark' © 1989 Martin Waddell,
illustrated by Barbara Firth. Reproduced by permission of
the publisher Walker Books., London.

Printed and bound in Great Britain by
Creative Print & Design (Wales), Ebbw Vale.

CONTENTS

1
BOOK POWER

A book about books?

Are books really so special that they deserve a book's worth of writing and drawing all to themselves? You bet they do!

Really. Books have been around for so long, and are so easy to take for granted, we tend to forget how amazing they actually are. A book can fill our heads with someone else's facts and fancies – someone who's far away, or dead, or completely imaginary. Yet, as we turn its pages, those facts and fancies come to life in a way that's utterly personal to us. For what you see, in your mind as you read, will never be identical with what I see – even if we're staring at exactly the same words.

For me, that's magical.

Books can make us hoot with laughter, burst into tears, or squirm with pain and pleasure. They can teach us about anything and everything – from Acrobatics to Zoology. They're brain-boosting, universe-exploring, time-shifting bundles of endless possibility.

AN EARLY BOOKWORM

Abdul Kassem Ismael, Grand Vizier of Persia in the 10th century, had a collection of 117,000 manuscripts which he refused to leave behind when he travelled. They were therefore carried by a team of 400 camels... trained to walk in alphabetical order.

JOHANNES GUTENBERG
(1398–1468)

It was a German, Johannes Gutenberg, who first realised that cutting the letters of the alphabet in type, and re-using them over and over again, was a lot faster and more efficient than writing books by hand. Between 1450–55, Gutenberg produced the first book printed from type – a Bible with 42 lines to each page. He exhibited it – yes, really – at the Frankfurt Trade Fair in 1455.

Yet this handy, pocket-sized object doesn't need any power-source, never lets us down by crashing and lasts pretty nearly forever if we look after it properly.

The right book at the right time can open our eyes, warm our hearts and help us make our dreams come true... yet stay entirely private while it does so.

THE LIBRARY OF CONGRESS

Situated in Washington USA, this is one of the world's great libraries. In 1995 alone (exactly 500 years after Gutenberg's Bible), 359,437 new books were added to its already vast collection. Clearly, the printing press had made its mark!

No wonder there's a lot of them about. Last year, we published over 8,000 new ones in the United Kingdom alone. Some had a print-run of just a few hundred copies, others flopped off the press by the million.

And that was just books for children!

If we're counting those for adults as well, each one with a title trying hard to be different from all the others, then there were more than a hundred thousand new publications altogether.

It was much the same the year before. Not to mention the year before that… and so on.

Meanwhile in other countries…

Yes, maybe we'd better pause a moment. Even a book-lover like me is beginning to feel a little faint. Luckily, another thing you can do with a book is to fan yourself, very gently, till you've built up the strength to move on to the next chapter.

2
FUN FOR ONE

Perhaps the saddest reader of all is someone who can read but never actually gets round to it. It's as if he, or she, hasn't discovered the best possible reason for picking up a book:

What's that?   SHEER ENJOYMENT

Of course, the lovely thing about bookish enjoyment is that it can happen anywhere and at any time – even when you're utterly alone. It's gloriously private and personal.

But how can I be sure that a book which is fun for me will be just as much fun for you? Here are five excerpts from some of the books I like best. I've chosen them because they're favourites of mine, but you may not agree with my selection at all.

So I can choose favourites of my own?

Exactly. Feel free to swop each of my examples for one of yours… Here's my first choice – it features a dad having a rant:

He was in full blast. Lydia and Christopher stood in sullen silence, while Natalie looked weepy and confused.

'I've sat through as many boring old child health clinics and grisly play groups in church halls as she has, I assure you. I've iced your birthday cakes, and wallpapered your bedrooms.' He banged his chest. 'I was even the sodding tooth fairy! Oh, yes. Make no mistake, I did as much as she did. You are my children as much as hers!'

Lydia and Christopher glowered, deeply indignant at the lecture, and smarting particularly at its implications of ownership. Natalie stood with her eyes lowered, inspecting her thumbs. She hadn't realised that before, about the tooth fairy…

It's from Anne Fine's novel, MADAME DOUBTFIRE. This is a serious scene, obviously. Yet a part of me can't help grinning as I read it. Maybe it reminds me of my own tooth fairy experiences. Or of my own dad

BUTTERED BOOKS

According to Charles Lamb (1775-1834), a new book can't match one we've handled over and over again. 'A book reads the better,' he wrote, 'which is our own, and has been so long known to us, that we know the topography of its blots, and dog's ears, and can trace the dirt in it to having read it at tea with buttered muffins.'

in full flow. Maybe it's Natalie's sudden insight which is so funny. Whatever it is, and it may be all three, everyday life seems more amusing than ever.

Other writers who can depict families so vividly are Tony Bradman, Adèle Geras, Philippa Pearce and Jean Ure. But remember, that's only my opinion!

Here's another kind of writing altogether:

When the sun goes down
and the moon comes up
and the old swing creaks
in the dark,
that's when we go
to the park,

me and Loopy
  and Little Gee,
    all three.

Softly down the staircase,
through the haunty hall,
trying to look
small,
me and Loopy
  and Little Gee,
    we three.

It's shivery
out in the dark
on our way to the park,
down dustbin alley,
past the ruined mill,
so still,
just me and Loopy
  and little Gee,
    just three.

Oo-er! Though this comes from a picture book text, Martin Waddell's THE PARK IN THE DARK, it reads more like verse than prose because it's the rhythm that makes it work – read it aloud if you don't believe me. Instantly I'm reminded of poets such as Roger McGough, Judith Nicholls, Michael Rosen and Kit Wright, not to mention the sheer creepiness of authors like Jack Prelutsky and R.L. Stine.

And notice how cleverly Martin Waddell makes it feel as if his night adventure is actually happening to us, not just his three cuddly toys. He does this by repeating that it's me and Loopy and Little Gee who are out on the prowl.

ASTRID LINDGREN
(born 1907)

As the author of PIPPI LONGSTOCKING, the BULLERBY and KARLSON books, THE BROTHERS LIONHEART, RONIA THE ROBBER'S DAUGHTER and many others, Astrid Lindgren has sold more than forty million copies in over sixty countries – making her, probably, the most translated author in the world. Is she also the most popular?

Well, in Germany alone 15 primary schools are named after her. And in Sweden, her birthplace, her witty complaint about her high taxes had the nation rocking with laughter. A little later, the government was voted out of office.

Beat that E. Blyton, R. Dahl and J. K. Rowling!

Crafty stuff.

Mind you, it's easy to feel involved when the words ringing in our head seem so special as well as so natural:

> Once again that sad winsome look came into the BFG's eyes. 'Words,' he said, 'is oh such a twitch-tickling problem to me all my life. So you must simply try to be patient and stop squibbling. As I am telling you before, I know exactly what words I am wanting to say, but somehow or other they is always getting squiff-squiddled around.'
>
> 'That happens to everyone,' Sophie said.
>
> 'Not like it happens to me,' the BFG said. 'I is speaking the most terrible wigglish.'
>
> 'I think you speak beautifully,' Sophie said.
>
> 'You do?' cried the BFG, suddenly brightening. 'You really do?'
>
> 'Simply beautifully,' Sophie repeated.

Haven't we all suffered moments of squiff-squiddling when we've tried to say something important?

In this extract from Roald Dahl's THE BFG, it's hard to know which part is more fun to play – the cool and brave little Sophie or the bumbling, kindly giant who seems so much sillier and wiser than most adults.

Luckily, with the wonderful wigglish of Roald Dahl, we can do both. Of course, he's assisted by the splendid pictures of his illustrator Quentin Blake – just as Martin Waddell is helped by Barbara Firth's drawing of Loopy, Little Gee and 'me'. Remember, books have been about pictures as well as words right from the beginning.

Not that wigglish is always the best option. Sometimes, plain English will do very nicely:

> Nothing could stop me. As if I were alone, back in the corner of the playground, I chested the ball up. It hung in the air and, for that second, it seemed as if the entire stadium was holding its breath. It began to fall.
>
> I pulled my favourite left foot, glanced up at the target – and let fly.
>
> It was as if all the strength and will in my body was being channelled through that foot, as if something superhuman was making contact with the ball. The result wasn't really a kick at all. It was a detonation, a controlled explosion of power. A force of nature.
>
> I looked up. The ball was in the back of the net. The Spurs keeper hadn't moved.

This is my favourite moment from Terence Blacker's THE TRANSFER. It's a story in which a bit of computer hocus-pocus allows an ordinary, everyday kid to become a world-class footballer.

But these extracts only scratch the surface. What about science fiction, historical novels, myths, legends and fairy stories? Well, I did say you might need to come up with choices of your own.

WHICH WITCH?

...or wizard, perhaps. The makers of magic have always been well represented in children's books, from Merlin in T. H. White's THE ONCE AND FUTURE KING to J. K. Rowling's HARRY POTTER. Here are a few others you may have come across: Jill Murphy's THE WORST WITCH, Kaye Umansky's PONGWIFFY, Humphrey Carpenter's MR MAJEIKA, Roald Dahl's THE WITCHES, Terence Blacker's MS WIZ and Ursula le Guin's A WIZARD OF EARTHSEA.

These passages are just a taster of the different worlds a book can bring alive for us – in a way which puts us right at the centre of the action. A person who can read, but doesn't, is rather like a wizard who owns a magic wand but somehow never gets round to waving it.

A magic wand?

Now, that reminds me...

Harry was several streets away before he collapsed onto a low wall in Magnolia Crescent, panting from the effort of dragging his trunk. He sat quite still, anger still surging through him, listening to the frantic thump of his heart.

But after ten minutes alone in the dark street, a new emotion overtook him: panic. Whichever way he looked at it, he had never been in a worse fix. He was stranded, quite alone, in the dark Muggle world, with absolutely nowhere to go. And the

worst of it was, he had just done serious magic, which meant that he was almost certainly expelled from Hogwarts.

I recognise this street exactly. I can see every detail of it in my mind as it stretches away in both directions. I recognise the feeling of being stranded, too, from the time I once got lost while carol-singing with the Cubs. Come to think of it, I recognise the boy as well. He's amazingly familiar...

It's Harry Potter!

Correct, though while I was reading this extract from J. K. Rowling's HARRY POTTER AND THE PRISONER OF AZKABAN, I couldn't help pretending his name was Harry Powling. And I bet millions of other readers have done the same as they immersed themselves in Harry's escapades.

This ability to draw the reader into a book is seen most clearly in stories and novels – what we call fiction. But a writer of factual books, sometimes called non-fiction, wants just the same thing. After all, every book – including THE BOOK ABOUT BOOKS – must keep the reader turning the page. Be careful, though. If you think books should always be cosy and safe, you'd better not turn over now.

Aaargh!

3
WORDS CAN BE DANGEROUS

Speaking your mind, especially in print, can seriously damage your popularity. And your health. Some pretty famous names have found this out the hard way.

Back in the sixteenth century, Galileo Galilei wrote a book called DIALOGUE CONCERNING THE TWO CHIEF WORLD SYSTEMS. In this he supported the idea that the earth went round the sun, challenging the belief at the time that the sun went round the earth. A year later, despite being well-known

CHOOSING YOUR OWN READING

Perhaps the wisest words on this subject were written by W.H. Auden (1907–73) in his poem 'Reading':

'Some books are undeservedly forgotten: None are undeservedly remembered.'

Enough said?

as one of the greatest astronomers who had ever lived, he had to make this announcement about his book:

'... with sincere and unfeigned faith,
I abjure, curse and detest the aforesaid
errors and heresies.'

Had he changed his mind?

Not a bit. He was being bullied by the Church which, in those days, wasn't at all keen on people thinking for themselves.

A century or so later, Daniel Defoe wasn't let off so easily. Nearly twenty years before he wrote his famous novel, ROBINSON CRUSOE, he published a pamphlet called SHORTEST WAY WITH DISSENTERS. It was meant to be funny – a tongue-in-cheek suggestion that people like himself, who refused to agree with 'official' religion, should be killed (the 'shortest' way to deal with them). The authorities didn't get the joke, and he ended up pilloried and in prison.

And it's not only your words that can get you into trouble – reading someone else's words could also cause problems. Take William Shakespeare for example – was he secretly a Catholic? In the England of the first Queen Elizabeth, Catholics were sentenced to death. Yet years after Shakespeare's death, a Catholic

pamphlet called TESTAMENT OF THE SOUL was found hidden in the rafters of his family home in Stratford, Warwickshire. Experts claim it was probably put there by Shakespeare's father when the playwright was in his teens... and liable to be sent to the scaffold, along with every other member of the household, if he'd been caught reading it.

Scary stuff.

But this all happened in the olden days, of course. Nothing like it could possibly happen in more recent times... isn't that right?

Wrong!

Writing books that offend important people is just as risky today as it's ever been. For Alexander Solzhenitsyn it meant a twenty-year exile from Russia when his book THE GULAG ARCHIPELAGO (1974) dared criticise the Soviet Government. In America, meanwhile, where freedom of speech is supposed to be guaranteed by law, they have an annual BANNED BOOKS WEEK to remind everyone about the titles they aren't allowed to read – because some administrator, politician or pressure group objects to what the authors are saying.

Perhaps the worst of recent cases concerns a British writer living in London. It began on February 14th, 1989 – St Valentine's Day, but there was nothing loving or jokey about the card Salman Rushdie received. He called it 'my funny Valentine'. The sender was the Ayatollah Khomeini, the religious leader of Iran. He'd issued a fatwah – a sort of official decree – which offered more than a million pounds to anyone who would kill Salman Rushdie along with everyone else involved in the publication of his novel THE SATANIC VERSES.

Because of one chapter, apparently, in which Rushdie describes a madman having a nightmare and making rude remarks about the Prophet Mohammad, the founder of the Muslim religion.

In the months that followed, Rushdie's Norwegian publisher was shot dead, his Japanese translator also lost his life and his Italian translator was badly injured. To keep himself safe, Rushdie was forced into heavily-guarded hiding for almost ten years. Eventually, after the murder of several of their own writers for disagreeing with government policy, the Iranians lifted the fatwah in September 1998.

Are Salman Rushdie's troubles over, then?

Let's hope so. But maybe it's still too soon to be sure.

In comparison, writers for children rarely cause such a stir. This said, they've always had to keep a wary eye on the opinions of other adults who take a keen interest in children's reading. All too often this takes the form of rubbishing the stories and poems children actually enjoy. For example, in the eighteenth century the writer Mrs Sarah Trimmer complained about the popularity of fairy tales because they 'fill the heads of children with confused notions of wonderful and supernatural events'.

Er... yes. Isn't that what they're supposed to do?

FORBIDDEN READING

In 411 BC, rulers in Athens banned all books by Protagoras; in 303 BC, Diocletian banned all Christian books in Rome; in 213 BC, the emperor Shih Huan-ti banned every book in China... just three examples of the burning of books by leaders who feared that reading makes people think for themselves.

Ancient history?

Not a bit. Jump forward a couple of millennia to our own era...

On May 10th 1933 in Berlin, the Nazis burned 20,000 books they happened to disagree with. In 1966, after four centuries in operation, the Catholic Index of Forbidden Books was finally discontinued. In 1980, parents in Tennessee tried to ban CINDERELLA, GOLDILOCKS and THE WIZARD OF OZ for religious reasons. In 1981, General Pinochet, who was then President of Chile, took against DON QUIXOTE on the grounds that it was critical of people like... well, General Pinochet.

For a gripping account of how Mark Twain's HUCKLEBERRY FINN was condemned as politically incorrect in an American High School, read Nat Hentoff's story THE DAY THEY CAME TO ARREST THE BOOK (1988).

DICKENS AND THE FAIRIES

A century and a half ago, the great novelist Charles Dickens was much amused by attempts to clean up the popular fairy tales – not least by his own illustrator George Cruikshank. In response, he wrote an article called 'Frauds on the Fairies'. Published in the magazine 'Household Words' in October 1853, it contains a marvellous spoof of CINDERELLA.
In it, she's described as 'a member of the Juvenile Bands of Hope when she was only four years of age'. Nowadays we have a phrase for the kind of fusspottiness Dickens was mocking: political correctness.

Another way of interfering is to draw up a list of 'significant' or 'recommended' books or authors. In the late 1980s, a new framework for teaching called the National Curriculum did just this. Thankfully it was dropped after howls of protest from librarians, teachers, authors and children themselves – most of whom were furious about being told what they should be reading.

Admittedly, there's another side to the story in both cases. What worried Sarah Trimmer was the number of people who really did believe in fairies and magic at the time she was writing. And the education advisers were quite genuine in their anxiety to extend children's reading. With books, though, sticking to lists is almost always a big mistake. They tend to leave out the fun and the messiness – the need, that is, for our book choices to be as personal and quirky as we are. In the end, it doesn't matter how 'good' a book is if it's just not right for us. Similarly, it doesn't much matter how 'bad' a book is if that's the one we fancy at the time.

On the whole, it seems best to let readers make up their own minds. Is Maurice Sendak's WHERE THE WILD THINGS ARE too scary for six-year-olds? That was the opinion of some critics when it was first published in 1967. What they forgot is that many children – and adults, too – like being a little bit scared. Over thirty years later, we recognise it as one of the greatest picture books ever.

So it's always worth watching out for the children's books which cause a great fuss amongst adults. These are likely to be the most eye-opening reads of all. BROTHER IN THE LAND by Robert Swindells is an honest account of nuclear war, for instance. Judy Blume's FOREVER is just as truthful about teenage sex and Melvin Burgess, in JUNK, gives the low-down –

BRIGGS THE BOGEYMAN

If you think it's just words that are considered dangerous, then you're wrong. Raymond Briggs' picture book, THE SNOWMAN, made him hugely popular... as did his FATHER CHRISTMAS books. With children, that is. But parents were nervous about a Santa who was so grumpy and so ordinary. FUNGUS THE BOGEYMAN left them even more nervous. So did WHEN THE WIND BLOWS and THE IRON LADY AND THE TIN POT GENERAL, for older readers, which both have an anti-war theme. As for ETHEL AND ERNEST, his graphic novel about his own parents, don't read it unless you're prepared to burst into tears – as I did when I got to the page which depicts the death of Raymond's father.

Another illustrator whose words and pictures make children laugh and parents tut-tut is Babette Cole.

---

and very low-down it is – on drugs. No wonder all three provoked demands that they should be banned.

You'd think we'd know better by now. Banning books often has a boomerang effect – it ends up promoting them. Librarians in the 1960s decided there were already far too many Enid Blyton titles on their shelves, so they stopped stocking new ones. Blyton herself wasn't much bothered. 'Good,' she's reported to have said. 'So the children will have to buy them, won't they.'

And her sales figures soared as a result.

4
BOOKS FROM
THE BEGINNING

Stories, jokes and gossip existed long before books, of course. Probably, they're as old as language itself – speech being a vital part of what makes us different from animals. So we shouldn't be too surprised that, historically, books arrived fairly late on the human scene.

SILENT READING

Nowadays, most of us are pretty good at silent reading. To begin with, though, the written words were almost always read out loud. In the libraries of ancient Egypt, Greece and Rome there must have been a constant mumble from the readers – never mind the click of tablets or unfurling of scrolls. This was true everywhere until well into the Middle Ages. Readers who read without a sound, and without moving their lips, were exceptional. The soldiers of Alexander the Great, in the fourth century BC, were amazed to see him reading a letter from his mother in complete silence.

The first book designed specifically for children was published only two-and-a-half centuries ago in 1744. If this seems surprisingly recent, remember that the first-ever book was published only three centuries or so before that. Up until then, readers had to make do with manuscripts... books written and illustrated by hand, one-at-a-time. Not surprisingly, most of the people who read them were either rich and important or worked for rich and important people – as priests, or teachers or clerks who were paid to keep track of legal and money matters.

Actually, writing was probably invented for legal and financial reasons in the first place. From what we know, it seems to have happened about five millennia ago in Mesopotamia (now Iraq) with a few simple signs chipped into tablets made of clay. Pretty soon, traders must have seen the advantage of these tablets. They weren't just an aid to memory, they were a record in case anyone was tempted to remember only what suited them.

Paper, you say? Well, it would certainly make my shopping list lighter.

Imagine, though, carrying a lot of clay tablets about. No wonder the 'technology' of writing developed as the centuries went by – in Greece, Egypt and North Africa. Tablets gave way to papyrus (a kind of reed) which in turn gave way to parchment (the skin of a sheep or goat). This was much easier to handle, to store and to bind up into something we'd recognise as a book. By the time paper was invented, it was clear that writing was more than just useful.

Also, it could entertain...

The first books printed in English, by William Caxton in 1474, were all stories – THE HISTORIES OF TROYE, THE FABLES OF AESOP, REYNARD THE FOX and MORTE D'ARTHUR. These were read for fun – though none  of them was intended for children. For the next couple of hundred years, in fact, there were only three kinds of book for young readers: ABCs and other schoolbooks to help them learn, 'courtesy' books to make them polite and 'good godly' books to keep them safe from wickedness. In short, early books for children told children exactly what they should think and do.

So John Newbery's A PRETTY LITTLE POCKET BOOK, published in 1744, was like a breath of fresh air. As a collection of rhymes about children's games,

its main aim was to be enjoyable – for the children of the better-off, remember. The idea that everyone should learn to read was still a long way off.

Mind you, many a canny youngster of the time may have already discovered that books don't have to be worthy and dull. Rougher, ruder and much closer to the tales and gossip of ordinary people were the 'chapbooks' sold by travelling pedlars or chapmen. These were hugely popular but never quite respectable – rather like a cross between a comic and a tabloid newspaper today. Here, folk and fairy stories jostled with legendary heroes like Robin Hood, Dick Whittington and Sir Bevis of Hampton... alongside rhymes such as this:

> 'Little Robin Redbreast sat upon a pole
> Niddle noddle went his head, poop went his hole...'

But even John Newbery intended his books 'for the Instruction and the Amusement of Little Master Tommy and Pretty Miss Polly'. Instruction, please note, came first. After him, the growing band of writers for children – including Sarah Trimmer, James Parkinson and Maria Edgworth – at least felt the need to hold their reader's attention. By the 1820s, folk and fairy stories had made a comeback with the translation of GRIMM'S FAIRY TALES. By the 1840s, adult stories like THE ARABIAN NIGHTS had been adapted for children and there was even a special series for children called FELIX SUMMERLEY'S HOME TREASURY which was designed 'to cultivate the affections, fancy, imagination and taste of children'.

What, no mention of *instruction*?

No. Obviously, ideas about childhood had been changing. No longer were boys and girls simply regarded as men and women in miniature. Now they were seen to have interests and rights of their own. This was reflected in the characters authors chose to write about. Take Lewis Carroll's Alice in ALICE'S ADVENTURES IN WONDERLAND (1865) and THROUGH THE LOOKING GLASS (1871). She tells the most important adults of all, including a King and Queen, that 'you're nothing but a pack of cards'. Admittedly, this only happens in a dream, but after cheek like this, a certain kind of stuffiness was bound to have gone forever. In 1883, Robert Louis Stevenson's TREASURE ISLAND contained a villain called Long John Silver

Off with her free choice!

who's easily the most memorable person in the book. And by 1911, Frances Hodgson Burnett's THE SECRET GARDEN featured a main character she describes as 'disagreeable' – and she remains that way for most of the story!

Why, it was almost as if adults were at last beginning to write the books children really wanted to read.

Well... up to a point. By the first half of the 20th century, there were plenty of children in books who gave the impression that they might actually exist. It certainly helped, though, if you came from a wealthy sort of family. If, for instance, you had brothers and sisters similar to the Bastables in E. Nesbit's THE STORY OF THE TREASURE SEEKERS (1899), went

SORTES VERGILIANAE

This was a way of predicting the future based on the 'magic' of certain books – usually those of the Roman poet Virgil or The Bible. A page was opened at random and a line identified by throwing three dice. This told you your fortune. Hocus Pocus? Well, sometimes, the result could be creepy. In an Oxford library, King Charles I turned up this line from Virgil: 'May he be harried in war by audacious tribes and exiled from his own land'. Seven years later, on January 30th 1649, it happened. After years of being harried by the audacious tribes of Oliver Cromwell, Charles was exiled permanently from his native land... because his head had been chopped off.

LEARNING TO READ

Nowadays, we take it for granted that almost everyone who lives in Britain will learn how to read. This wasn't the case till the Education Act of 1871, though. Before this, only Sweden had a population where most grown-ups could read – mainly because the Lutheran Church refused to marry them until they could.

to a school of the kind described by Frank Richards in his GREYFRIARS series (1908), played with toys of the kind owned by Christopher Robin in A. A. Milne's WINNIE THE POOH (1926) or went sailing in the holidays like the children in Arthur Ransome's SWALLOWS AND AMAZONS (1930), then you had nothing much to complain about. In almost every book you opened, you'd have felt you were meeting close friends.

Pity they left out almost everyone else... especially those who had to cope with being poor and ill-educated.

The truth is, that for many years, comics and magazines like THE BEANO and DANDY and WIZARD and HOTSPUR probably offered a much better reflection of the lives of most children than books did. And it wasn't till your parents were growing up that the real breakthrough came. Nowadays, we tend to take it for granted that we'll find someone like ourselves in the books we read whatever our class or race or creed. How did this come about?

Partly from other keen readers, of course – the parents and librarians and teachers who were determined to share the pleasure they got from books with as many people as possible. Why shouldn't all children be represented in books, they wanted to know. As a result, writers like E. W. Hildick, born in 1925, actually began to write about most children, not just the privileged few. His character, Jim Starling, starred in a number of stories in the 1950s and 60s and was one of the first 'ordinary' heroes.

But a key factor, once again, was technology.

In the 1950s and 60s, following their success with adult readers, paperback books became increasingly available for children. Paperbacks were lighter, handier... and cheaper. Young readers had never had a better chance to choose titles for themselves. For the first time ever, in fact, they didn't have to be rich to

PENGUINS AND PUFFINS

Paperback books, in one form or another, have been around since the seventeenth century. Originally a development of the booklets and ballads sold by chapmen, they were intended for 'outdoor' or 'travelling' reading. On June 30th 1935, this changed for ever with the publication of the first ten Penguins by Allen Lane in London. They cost sixpence a volume – the cheapest a quality book had ever been. Soon paperbacks became serious competition for hardbacks.

In 1961, Lane launched Puffins, a series of paperback books for children. They were edited, with huge success, by Kaye Webb. Today, all the major publishing houses have a paperback division.

build up a personal collection of books to suit their own tastes and preferences.

For some adults this was scary.

Suppose children opted for rubbish? Or only for one kind of writing? What if they completely ignored the sort of story or poem or information book which might stretch them a bit?

Such questions caused much shaking of heads among some critics and educationalists. Suddenly, a new complaint began to be heard... that, these days, too many books are being published for children.

Which books should be dumped, though?

We can guess who'd do the choosing, and what the likely outcome would be. Imagine, for instance, a campaign to make children eat more healthily by closing down every 'junk' food outlet. Why would a campaign for 'healthy' reading – by closing down every 'junk' story or poem outlet – work any better?

Besides, how can we be sure which books are 'junk' and which are 'healthy'?

The truth is, we should celebrate the volume and variety of children's reading today – from junk books to gourmet books. Yes, we need a balanced diet in our reading, but the best way to achieve that, for both adults and children, is to be well informed, keep an open mind...

... and take risks.

5
BOOKS THAT LAST FOR EVER

A book is dead until someone starts reading it. If it's really old, then the voice you can hear in your head as you scan the pages may have been silent for years.

Some books, though, refuse to let time shut them up. They've gone on echoing in reader's minds ever since they were first written. These are the stories and poems which, according to the seventeenth century writer John Milton, we won't 'willingly let die'.

We call them classics.

Of course, this doesn't mean we're guaranteed to like them, or must force ourselves to read them at all costs. After all, most of us would become quite sniffy if someone insisted on telling us what music to enjoy or which television programmes to watch. The same applies to books. The best way to kill a title stone dead is to demand that everyone gives it a go regardless of personal feelings and preferences. That's why the poet Adrian Mitchell began his collection BALLOON LAGOON with this warning:

'None of these poems or any other work by Adrian Mitchell is to be used in connection with any examination or test whatsoever. But I'm glad if people who like them read them aloud, sing them, dance them or act them in school. And even happier if they choose to learn any of them by heart.'

He wanted readers to encounter his poetry freely and enjoyably – not in circumstances where they had no choice.

Suppose, on the other hand, there was a tune so amazing that someone, somewhere in the world was bound to be whistling it... no matter how long ago it was composed.

JOHN MILTON... AND PHILIP PULLMAN

The seventeenth-century poet John Milton is famous for his long and learned narrative poems now mostly studied by scholars. Not an obvious source for a children's writer, perhaps. Yet Philip Pullman's HIS DARK MATERIALS trilogy was inspired by Milton's PARADISE LOST, a tale about how Evil came into the world when a group of angels rebelled against God. The first book, NORTHERN LIGHTS', was published to great acclaim in 1995. Two years later came the second, THE SUBTLE KNIFE and the third, THE AMBER SPYGLASS, was eagerly awaited.

Wouldn't you be eager to find out about it?
Sooner rather than later?

That's how we should regard a classic – as something so extraordinary we'd be selfish if we didn't give as many people as possible the chance to encounter it. Luckily, most 'classic' titles are pretty hard to avoid:

- Because they tend to exist in a number of different versions, eg. as pop-ups, comic-strips, picture books or in specially illustrated new editions.

- Because, eventually, they almost all go multi-media, and end up as movies, stage plays, serials on radio or television, cartoon-films and even ballets and operas.

Beware, though...

AN ADAPTATION OF A CLASSIC, HOWEVER BRILLIANT, DOESN'T OFFER THE SAME EXPERIENCE AS THE BOOK ON WHICH IT IS BASED.

Unless you check out the original, you may miss the very magic which made it special in the first place.

Was it the pace and timing of the story, for instance? The fascination of the characters? The wit or power of the author's style? The way the book wised us up, or shifted our opinions or made us burst out laughing or sniffle into our hankies?

At least one of these aspects must be utterly out-standing if the book has gone on and on pleasing readers.

But don't imagine that 'classic' means the same as 'perfect'. This simply isn't true – whether it's for children or adults. A good example here is Kenneth Grahame's THE WIND IN THE WILLOWS. This is the story of a group of humanised animals who live on a river bank. But is it intended as a tale for youngsters or for dreamy old buffers like Kenneth Grahame himself? Do the slapstick chapters involving the lovable but roguish Mr Toad really fit in with those about Mole and Ratty? And how come Mr Toad him-self is sometimes big enough to drive a real car and sometimes as small as... well, a toad?

So the book's a bit of a mess, is it?

Maybe so. But who cares about any of these problems once Kenneth Grahame has transported us to a place like The Wild Wood?

Here's how it feels to Mole:

'Everything was very still now. The dusk advanced on him steadily, rapidly, gathering in behind and before; and the light seemed to be draining away like floodwater.

Then the faces began...'

After this comes the whistling and the pattering.

By the time Mole panics and rushes deeper and deeper into the trees we're too busy running with him to worry about anything the novel gets wrong. Kenneth Grahame has bewitched us by what he gets so thrillingly right.

Classics, then, are books so brilliant they blind us to their faults – even after we've worked out exactly what these faults are. By today's standards, they may even be racist, sexist or horribly snobbish. And it's important we recognise such weaknesses. But it's even more important to notice the standards these books set so spectacularly... not just for their time but beyond it.

Beyond it? Yes. Strictly speaking, we can only really be certain we're reading a classic if it's survived from a former age. Plenty of books which were hugely popular and fashionable when

---

SPIN-OFFS

Once a book becomes seriously famous, there's a chance to sell the merchandising rights and produce 'spin-offs'. This is the name given to the mugs, pencils, postcards, tea towels, pyjamas or whatever that carry the logo of a famous title or character. Some characters even have dolls and puppets made of them. Spin-offs can be worth a lot of money, and A. A. Milne's WINNIE THE POOH is a good example. In 1999, the Walt Disney Corporation renewed their merchandising licence to sell Pooh products. For this, they paid the heirs of Milne's estate more than forty million pounds.

---

your parents were young are now nearly forgotten. However, some of them refuse to disappear:

NOT NOW BERNARD – David McKee

THE IRON MAN – Ted Hughes

TOM'S MIDNIGHT GARDEN – Philippa Pearce

Here we have a picture book, a fantasy and a time-shift novel which it's hard to believe will ever be bettered.

But these are just my choices. What are your suggestions for classics-in-waiting? Pat Hutchins's ROSIE'S WALK, perhaps? Jenny Nimmo's THE SNOW SPIDER? Michael Rosen's QUICK LET'S GET OUT OF HERE?

Maybe you'd opt for a different title by these authors – or for another set of authors altogether.

If you and your friends have read a particular book

COMPULSORY READING

Here are fifty so-called 'classics', every child ought to have read by the age of eleven... according to The Times newspaper in 1988 (in order of popularity):

Ages 3-7
Just So Stories
Rudyard Kipling
The Tale of Peter Rabbit
Beatrix Potter
Charlotte's Web
E.B. White
The Very Hungry Caterpillar
Eric Carle
The World of Pooh
A. A. Milne
Dogger
Shirley Hughes
Mr Gumpy's Outing
John Burningham
Where the Wild Things Are
Maurice Sendak
Each Peach Pear Plum
Allan and Janet Ahlberg
Mr Magnolia
Quentin Blake
Now We Are Six
A. A. Milne
Rosie's Walk
Pat Hutchins
Where's Spot?
Eric Hill

Ages 8-11
The Wind in the Willows
Kenneth Grahame

The Hobbit
J.R.R. Tolkien
Tom's Midnight Garden
Philippa Pearce
The BFG
Roald Dahl
The Iron Man
Ted Hughes
The Secret Garden
Frances Hodgson Burnett
A Christmas Carol
Charles Dickens
The Lion, the Witch and the Wardrobe
C.S.Lewis
Alice in Wonderland
Lewis Carroll
Complete Nonsense Book of Edward Lear
Edward Lear
The Ghost of Thomas Kempe
Penelope Lively
The Silver Sword
Ian Serraillier
Stig of the Dump
Clive King
The Stone Book
Alan Garner
The Treasure Seekers
E. Nesbit

*The Turbulent Term of
Tyke Tyler*
Gene Kemp
*The Wolves of
Willoughby Chase*
Joan Aiken

Ages 12-18
Eagle of the Ninth
Rosemary Sutcliff
Treasure Island
R.L. Stevenson
Brother in the Land
Robert Swindells
Smith
Leon Garfield
The Machine Gunners
Robert Westall
1984
George Orwell
Carrie's War
Nina Bawden
Catcher in the Rye
J.D. Salinger
The Box of Delights
John Masefield

The Diary of Anne Frank
Anne Frank
The Earthsea Trilogy
Ursula le Guin
Emil and the Detectives
Erich Kastner
Goldengrove
Jill Paton Walsh
*The Adventures of
Huckleberry Finn*
Mark Twain
Jane Eyre
Charlotte Brontë
*The Hound of the
Baskervilles*
A. Conan Doyle
Lord of the Flies
William Golding
Moonfleet
J. Meade Falkner
The Owl Service
Alan Garner
Pride and Prejudice
Jane Austen

What? You've missed several of these? Don't
worry, so had most of us when we were eleven.
The real danger of lists like this, which are almost
always compiled by adults, is that children may be
forced to read books that aren't quite right for
them at the time... and end up being put
off them for ever.

to bits, can't imagine ever forgetting it and are convinced it compares well with some of the great titles of the past... then maybe you've managed to identify a legitimate classic. Don't hold your breath, though.

Only time will tell.

6
CREATING
A BOOK

Where do an author's ideas come from?

Some people have romantic notions about this. They think it's entirely a matter of inspiration – a bolt from the blue as it were. This hits the author unexpectedly and forces him or her to work furiously, in a sort of trance, hardly stopping for food or drink until the last page is finished.

Well, maybe that's true for some writers. But I've never actually met one. Most authors are much more down-to-earth. They regard storytelling as a job – a wonderful job, admittedly, but still a job. If they sat around waiting to be struck by inspiration, the chances are they'd starve to death or end up as nervous wrecks.

Perhaps the best answer to the question 'What does it take to be a writer?' was given by the novelist P. G. Wodehouse. 'It's simple,' he told a newspaper reporter. 'You keep your bum on a chair.'

In other words, you can't avoid the long, hard slog.

INVENTING ROOMS

Books can be written anywhere. It's one of the great bonuses of being an author. Most writers have a favourite place to work, though. Everyone knows about Roald Dahl's writing hut in his orchard (Philip Pullman and Alan Durant also write in garden sheds) but here are some private spaces you may not know about...

BRIAN MOSES – an extension at the back of his house.

BENJAMIN ZEPHANIAH – upstairs front room.

IAN BECK – downstairs front room.

BERLIE DOHERTY – a small barn behind her house.

CELIA REES – in the biggest room in her house.

TONY BRADMAN – has just moved from his dining-room to a back bedroom.

Where each author feels most comfortable, in fact. Notice that none of these places is really unusual. There's probably somewhere just like it in your house where you can do some writing of your own!

Certainly, inspiration is part of the story.

Don't we all get moments when the creative juices are flowing? Or when a brilliant idea suddenly arrives out of nowhere? A seven-year-old once described this very accurately when she was asked how she'd come up with a poem for her school magazine. 'I got a kick in the mind,' she explained. 'And it said itself.'

But who'd want to earn a living by relying on kicks in the mind? Not me, that's for sure.

In my case, a book can be triggered by almost any-thing. Sometimes, it's a real-life incident. The HARRY books, for instance, are all based on events that actually happened to me or my family. With A RAZZLE-DAZZLE-RAINBOW, on the other hand, my starting point was the phrase, 'Ding-Dong-Curly-Whirly-Cuckoo-Boing', which I heard in a London primary school. On another occasion, I was fascinated by a girl who loved dressing up in a dog costume – this became the mini-series of four books called MY SISTER'S NAME IS ROVER.

For me, inspiration isn't something that hits you at all. It's much more like a peg on which you realise you can hang a story… a story you spin for yourself from memories or dreams, or your own imagination. That's where the hard slog comes in.

The experience of Shirley Hughes, with her famous picture book DOGGER, is probably very typical. In the story, Dogger is a much-loved soft toy who goes missing, and as Shirley explains, 'He literally fell out of a cupboard I was tidying. He belonged to one of my sons... and I suddenly remembered all the fuss it caused when he got lost.'

After this came weeks and weeks of getting the story into shape. 'While I'm writing the words, my brain is already filling up with pictures. Then comes a 'rough'. I draw this very fast with felt pen or pencil. I'm really excited as I do it. The coloured pictures take much longer than the rough. Colour gives the story its mood... but I mustn't lose that excitement.'

Sometimes, the process involved in writing and drawing a book isn't at all straightforward. This was the case with Anthony Browne's PIGGYBOOK – his sharp and funny satire about a family of three selfish males and one exploited female: 'I set to work on the illustrations but, after a while, I became unhappy about the way the pigs looked. I felt the ending of the story just wasn't right. In the end, I decided to abandon the book when I was halfway through it. I put the illustrations in a drawer and got on with other work. About two years later, I was idly looking at them

---

WRITING IN BED

Reading in bed is one thing. But what about writing in bed? Late in her life, the French novelist Colette perfected this by inventing a bed-raft in her Paris apartment where she slept, ate, entertained, phoned, read... and wrote.

52

again, when suddenly I thought of a much better ending... and a new way to draw the pigs.'

Clearly, for a professional, the creative process calls for stamina as well as bright ideas.

Something else is involved, too. Quentin Blake, Britain's first ever Children's Laureate and the author-illustrator of books like MR MAGNOLIA, CLOWN and ZAGAZOO, describes his thinking approach as 'more instinct than thinking'. 'It's very hard to know whether I've got the idea for a finished drawing in my mind's eye already – or whether I'm making it up as I go along. Even if I do start off with an idea of the way a drawing should look, the chances are that as soon as I start – once the pen starts making the marks – it'll create something I couldn't possibly have decided in advance.'

The same sort of instinct, rather than straight-forward thinking, seems to apply to writers as well as illustrators. Here's Helen Cresswell who wrote the hilarious BAGTHORPE series:

'With most of my books I simply write a title and a sentence, and I set off and the road just leads to where it finishes... I often put off starting because it's scary in a way.'

Does this mean all forward-planning is bad?

Not quite.

If only to ward off that scariness, most writers need some sense of a book's direction. Gillian Cross, author of THE DEMON HEADMASTER and THE GREAT ELEPHANT CHASE, copes in this way:

'Before I start a novel I'll write a synopsis and talk it through with the editor. Usually at that stage I haven't the faintest idea what is going into the book. I often know the beginning scene, and the area it's going to be about, and the feel of it... I won't look at the synopsis again unless I get really stuck – because, in a way, the plan interferes with the writing of the

GHOST WRITERS

No, these aren't authors from beyond the grave. It's the name we give to the writers who help non-writers, such as sports personalities or politicians, tell their story – so don't be too amazed if your favourite pop star writes a surprisingly readable book. Probably he, or she, has been assisted by a 'ghost'.

book, and I need to start a story with no shape and to find out what it is as I go along.'

So a synopsis needs to know its place. A good story depends on believable characters as well as a gripping plot. And what kind of character doesn't contain some element of surprise – even for the writer who's doing the inventing? Jacqueline Wilson, whose books include DOUBLE ACT and THE ILLUSTRATED MUM has commented on this:

'Although I would know vaguely what I was going to do, I didn't really want to detail all the ins and outs of the story because I wanted to keep it alive, and also I might have wanted to do it quite differently when I got down to writing it...'

These remarks are fairly representative of authors generally. What most writers seem to rely on is a combination of hunch and concentration. They have an ability to fill their minds so vividly with the story they're telling that they can trust themselves to follow their noses without getting lost.

Different authors achieve this in different ways. Their procedures are strictly personal – where they write, when they write, how they write is entirely up to them. Most professionals agree, though, that it helps to have some sort of routine. As the playwright Noel Coward once remarked scathingly 'an amateur is someone who can only write when it's raining.'

In short, amateurs need to feel like writing before they do it. Professionals don't. They get on with it because it's their job.

With non-fiction, as you'd expect, there's a shift in approach. Here, forward-planning is much more important. Now we're talking facts – and these must be chosen and organised. Neil Ardley, author of 101 GREAT SCIENTIFIC EXPERIMENTS and THE EYE-WITNESS GUIDE TO MUSIC, is adamant about this:

'Before I begin a book I'll know almost all the information that will be going into it – I have to. I couldn't write it otherwise.'

There are two other significant differences between non-fiction and fiction:

- Most information books are commissioned. This means a publisher has actually asked the author to write it – unlike most stories and poems which are written 'on spec' in the hope that a publisher will like them enough to publish them.

- Information books tend to involve more teamwork – the part played by the editor and the illustrator can now become as crucial as that of the writer.

Or even *more* crucial? Well, yes, according to Neil Ardley, also author of THE WAY THINGS WORK. He's full of admiration for his editor, David Burnie, whose job it was to 'hold the project together' and to 'clarify all those parts of your writing, and point out all the problem areas that you aren't aware of, because you're too close to see them.'

That vital, eh?

He reserves his highest praise, though, for the illustrator David Macaulay, whose drawings defined the overall approach and were 'the most vital ingredient in the book's success'.

Yes, but please don't mention this to Scoular Anderson who illustrated this book!

SCOULAR ANDERSON

A chance for Scoular to appear before your very eyes!

Fiction and non-fiction are not the same then, and can't be reduced to a single process. So be wary of people who tell you that writing a story or poem is just a matter of learning the tricks of the trade. This simply isn't true. You also need a bit of magic, like Quentin Blake's 'instinct'.

How, then, can you develop this instinct? The best, and the most enjoyable, way is to follow the example of just about every writer who's ever lived...

... and you read and read and read.

Eventually, as you absorb the voice behind other people's stories and poems, you'll begin asking yourself how your own voice sounds on the page.

After this, it's a matter of keeping your bum on that chair.

7
PUBLISHING
A BOOK

First, the bad news.

Every publishing company, large or small, has a whole stack of manuscripts from wannabe-writers. It's called 'the slush pile'. And the odds that your story will be picked from the pile and published are about three thousand-to-one against. So be prepared for disappointment.

Now the good news.

Some very famous authors suffered the same disappointment at the start of their careers. F. Scott Fitzgerald, whose novels THE GREAT GATSBY, TENDER IS THE NIGHT and THE LAST TYCOON make him one of the great writers of the twentieth century, is said to have papered his bathroom ceiling with rejection slips before his first book was accepted.

Amongst children's authors, consider the case of Richard Adams. His first book was rejected by fourteen different publishers before the fifteenth, Rex Collings, took a deep breath and said yes. It was called WATERSHIP DOWN. Soon afterwards, when the awards and sales figures began to arrive, there were fourteen publishers who felt rather cross with themselves.

But miracles do happen, remember.

About 25 years ago, a London teacher couldn't find the right sort of book for his inner-city pupils. So, over a period of 18 months, he wrote a set of short stories with the title DARE-DEVILS OR SCAREDY-CATS. Not knowing any publishers or agents, he was totally dependent on THE WRITERS' AND ARTISTS' YEARBOOK 1978, which listed every publishing outlet there was with a brief explanation of the kind of books each published. He sent his typescript to the very first children's publisher on the list: Abelard Schuman. Two months later, his book was accepted. Amazingly, Abelard had been looking for a book exactly like his.

> A fairy-tale come true?

Well, it certainly felt that way at the time. You see, at this very moment, you're holding that writer's 55th book in your hand.

Let's assume you've been just as lucky. A major publishing house has accepted a picturebook text you've written. You've signed a lengthy standard contract and you've banked the advance – you probably won't receive any more money until the book is published. But the good thing is that the money belongs to you. You'll keep it even if your book doesn't sell a single copy.

After this, you're in the hands of the experts:

The Editor

The **editor** checks your English, matches your words and pictures, and very tactfully suggests ways in which both can be improved. Trust editors – they've had a lot

> I'm the editor so you two can pipe down!

> THE BOOK ABOUT BOOKS

more experience than you. As soon as the text is finalised, it is loaded on to a disk and handed to the designer.

The Designer

The **designer's** job is to come up with a design for the front cover and to lay out the inside pages. This involves deciding on the typefaces and where the text is placed on each page. The designer also works directly with the **illustrator**. The illustrator provides rough illustrations that are checked by you, the editor and the designer. The illustrator then draws the final illustrations. Next the designer makes low resolution scans of the illustrations so that he can work with them on screen. He positions the text and illustrations on each page and prints out a final copy of the layouts with everything in place for you and the editor to take a last look.

The Production Manager

Once everything has been approved, the designer hands the disk containing the layouts and the original artwork to the **production manager** who sends it on to the repro (reproduction) house. At the repro house, the artwork is scanned using a powerful scanner that separates the artwork into four colours – cyan, magenta, yellow and black – ready for the printing process. The repro house sends the publishers a proof of the book so everyone can make sure the colours are accurate, and that all the text and pictures are in place.

The Printer

More technical stuff. Once the proof from the repro house has been approved, the disk containing the book is sent to the **printer** along with the proof. The information on the disc is then burnt on to photosensitive metal printing plates that are wrapped round a cylinder – one plate for each of the four main colours. The printing press prints on one side of the huge sheets of paper (normally 16 pages). The sheets are allowed to dry and then turned over and printed on the reverse. They are taken to the bindery where they

HELLO... AGAIN!

Some characters refuse to stay in one book. Joyce Lancaster Brisley's MILLY-MOLLY-MANDY, Joan G Robinson's TEDDY ROBINSON and Jean and Gareth Adamson's TOPSY AND TIM are just three long-lasting favourites who have all appeared in many books. Perhaps the greatest of them all, though, is Richmal Crompton's William Brown who was introduced in JUST WILLIAM in 1922, and stayed eleven years old till WILLIAM THE LAWLESS in 1970, thirty-seven books later – having starred in more than four hundred of the finest short stories for children ever written.

are folded and gathered into 16-page sections, called signatures. All books are made up of 16-page signatures – THE BOOK ABOUT BOOKS, for example, is 96 pages and contains six signatures. The signatures are trimmed and stitched, and bound with the book's cover. Finally the books are packed into crates ready for delivery to the warehouse.

Phew!

The whole process can take up to a year or more. No wonder it's such a relief, and so exciting, when you receive your 6 free copies of the book along with a note of congratulation from your publisher. And no wonder publishers have to choose so carefully from the typescripts they get sent. A wrong choice can cost them a lot of money.

Thank goodness there are less nerve-racking opportunities to get your stories and pictures published – as part of a classroom display, perhaps, or in your school magazine or maybe on the internet. If you tell yourself it's impossible for a kid like you to crack the hard-nosed world of professional publishing, though... you're in for a shock.

Back in 1992, a Wolverhampton girl called Caitlin Moran published a book called THE CHRONICLES OF NARMO. The best-selling author Terry Pratchett was so impressed with this, he commented 'Oh God, this good already and she's only sixteen.'

SERIES PUBLISHING

Children have always liked books which feature the same characters, the same kind of story/storytelling or are recognisable because they're aimed at particular groups of readers. Modern successes include BANANA BOOKS from Heinemann, JETS from A & C Black and GOOSEBUMPS from Scholastic. Adults are sometimes sniffy about series books... conveniently forgetting that crime novels, and historical fiction, are often just as popular with grown-ups for much the same reasons.

But it was worse than Terry Pratchett thought. In the same year, Stephen Pepler had illustrated a picturebook called STEPHEN'S HISTORY OF THE SAINTS... at the age of six. Even Stephen, though, was a bit long in the tooth compared with Jonathan Shelley in America. He wrote the text for WHEN THE DINOSAURS LIVED, published in 1989, when he was four-and-a-half.

Doesn't it makes you wonder how the rest of us filled in our time before we went to school?

PICTUREBOOK PARTNERS

One way to maintain a working relationship between author and illustrator is for the two to be married... like Colin and Jacqui Hawkins who produced SCHOOL, MONSTERS and DAFT DOG or Laurence and Catherine Anholt who brought us LOOK WHAT I CAN DO, ALL ABOUT YOU and THE MAGPIE SONG. But perhaps the most successful of all such husband-and-wife teams was Allen and Janet Ahlberg with their books HAPPY FAMILIES, EACH PEACH PEAR PLUM and THE JOLLY POSTMAN.

But do you know which one, out of each husband and wife team, wrote the story and which one drew the illustrations?
*Answers on page 94.

Not that an early start is essential for literary success. Far from it. Sometimes it helps to live a bit first. One of today's most popular tellers of animal tales – with more than a hundred titles to his credit and over six million copies sold – didn't publish his first book till he was 55 years old. He's the author of THE SHEEP-PIG (filmed as BABE), THE HODGE-HEG, THE ROUNDHILL and scores of other stories which draw on his experience as a countryman and farmer. The career of Dick King-Smith is a handy reminder that you're never too old to challenge the odds of the slush pile.

8
BUYING AND BORROWING

Buying a book has never been easier... or cheaper. There are three main outlets keen for your custom:

A traditional bookshop or book department.
A Bookclub or School Bookfair.
An internet company like amazon.co.uk
or bol.com.

Of course, it helps if you know the book you're looking for.

Here's where the ISBN comes in. ISBN stands for International Standard Book Number and you'll find it on the back cover of most books just above the bar code.

ISBNs apply world-wide and are a simple and effective way of pinpointing a particular edition of a particular title by a particular author...

... but not very memorably.

Imagine a conversation like this:

If this is how you talk about books then maybe you should get out a bit more.

Preferably as far as your nearest bookshop. Apart from a library (which we'll come to in a page or two) this is the best possible place to locate the book you're after. Alternatively, you can engage in one of the most enjoyable of all reading activities – browsing.

This number identifies the language group in which the book was first published – eg 0 for English in the UK, 1 for English in America or Australia, up to 5 digits for less international languages.

This is a check digit which tells computers if an ISBN has been entered wrongly.

ISBN 0-7136-5478-3

This number identifies the publisher – in this case A & C Black.

This identifies the book – here, the 5,478th A & C Black have published since ISBNs began. It's a book called THE BOOK ABOUT BOOKS. If you're holding the paperback version then it should read 5479.

Browsing in a bookshop is a kind of mooching with the mind – you take your brain for a stroll round other people's writing as you decide whether or not you fancy delving deeper. It's like having a lick at every flavour in an ice-cream parlour before you make your selection...

And however much you gorge yourself, you'll still have the 'food' in front of you.

This is where a bookshop scores over a Bookclub or School Bookfair (where the size of the bargain is all too often marred by the narrowness

Bliss!

of the choice). In a bookshop there's usually so much more on offer. And what you see are the books themselves, not just pictures of the covers.

Don't turn your nose up at second-hand book-shops, either. Crisp, new books are wonderful... but you'll find much the same selection in other shops on other High Streets. Spend an hour rummaging in a second-hand bookshop and you might find a fasci-nating, dusty, dog-eared old tome priced at less than a birthday card. And it may be the only copy that's available.

Or is it?

If someone's picked up the book of your dreams just ahead of you, don't despair. You can get expert help in tracking down another copy by consulting The Book Trust or the website www.bookfinder.com or a specialist company like Twiggers which will do your

COPYRIGHT

If you pretend someone else's writing is your own, you are likely to be accused of plagiarism. Publishing another person's work without their permission is piracy. Both offend the Copyright, Designs and Patents Act 1988 which protects authors from such literary theft. That's why you'll find something like this at the front of most books:

Text copyright © 2000 Chris Powling
Illustrations copyright © 2000 Scoular Anderson

You have been warned.

searching for you. Some bookshops also provide the same service – often free of charge or for a small fee on top of the purchase price.

Thanks to the internet, if a book can be located it almost certainly will be... also packed and despatched straight to your door. On the internet you'll find back-up information, such as details about a particular author, along with a range of other promotional material. No wonder bookshops are increasingly adding these services to their own speciality: the chance to check out a title at first hand before you've parted with your money.

Ah, yes... the question of money. Considering the hours of pleasure they bring, books really are terrific value. But they still have to be paid for. What if your pockets are empty or your reading-speed runs way ahead of your cash flow?

Don't despair. One hundred and fifty years ago, a special Act of Parliament empowered every town in Britain to sort out this problem once and for all.

How?

By setting up a Public Library.

A Public Library is one of the most amazing places on earth. Any person who lives locally can use it. It has trained staff to answer any queries and however many times you borrow the books you find there – old and new – it offers its basic services free of charge.

P.L.R.

For years, authors complained that no matter how many times one of their books was borrowed from Public libraries they never received a penny. This was finally put right in 1979 when parliament passed the Public Lending Right Act.

Since then, authors have received a payment – currently about two pence – for each borrowing. Libraries aren't able to keep track of every single copy of every single book. The figures are based on loans carefully monitored in a sample of libraries throughout Britain. The maximum amount authors can receive is £6,000. The money is paid in February each year.

The Authors' Licensing and Collecting Society, or ALCS, does a similar job with any copied, broadcast or recorded extracts from an author's work.

Different libraries will vary a bit in detail just as different schools do. But Abertillery Library, tucked away in Blaenau Gwent, South Wales, is probably typical of branch libraries all over the British Isles:

Number of users each year : 341,148
Number of hours open each year : 1,842
Number of borrowings each year : 492,759
Number of enquiries each year : 125,670

With such a workload a team of four librarians is kept permanently on the go. Along with its school visits, its competitions and meet-the-author sessions, its IT facilities and mobile library for taking books to borrowers in remote places (as well as a magazine called KID ZONE for its junior members) Abertillery Library strives to make reading fun. But that's not all. Books have to be bought, catalogued and shelved as

I'm Sue, and I'm one of the Library Managers. I work mainly with young readers.

well – not just for this branch but for other branches in the Blaenau Gwent area, too. This involves more specialist staffing:

At Abertillery, you can borrow up to ten titles at a time for up to three weeks. You can also take away five videos, five music items and a Play-station game (though

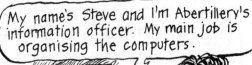

> My name's Steve and I'm Abertillery's information officer. My main job is organising the computers.

you're asked to return these within a week). And you can do all this as often as you like.

There's a small charge for the music items, but the books are absolutely free!

FIVE KEY FACTS
ABOUT LIBRARIES

- Earliest – founded in Babylonian Nineveh in 7th century BC.

- First public – opened in Athens in 330 BC.

- Statistics – 58% of Britons are library members, borrowing some 480 million books a year.

- Current cost – Britain's library service costs the price of a first class stamp per person per week.

- Popularity – visiting the library is the fourth most popular pastime in the UK, after going to pubs, restaurants and eating take-aways.

FINDING A LIBRARY BOOK

Fiction tends to be grouped in alphabetical order by the author's surname. Information books are usually grouped by subject. Most libraries use the Dewey Decimal Classification system for this which gives each subject a number code:

000 – 099	General Works	500 – 599	Science
100 – 199	Philosophy	600 – 699	Technology
200 – 299	Religion	700 – 799	Fine Arts
300 – 399	Social Studies	800 – 899	Literature
400 – 499	Languages	900 – 999	History & Geography

Beware, though. Many books defy exact classification. Jonathan Swift's GULLIVER'S TRAVELS could be filed under fiction, under Social Studies, under Literature, under History and Geography... or even as a forerunner of Science Fiction. If in doubt, ask a librarian.

A Public Library is a treasure-trove for book-lovers – except there's no dragon to keep you at bay. On the contrary, whether you're the smallest toddler or the grandest professor, you'll get the warmest of welcomes from the staff. What you'll also get is the feeling of being in touch. For libraries are changing all the time as society and technology changes. They give us a window on the world of reading with barely a single price-tag in sight.

If you're not a member already, join now.

9
MAKING BOOKS MATTER

A book locked up in a cage?

And children forbidden to buy it until school was over – with special arrangements to cope with the rush?

Yes, you've got it. The book was J. K. Rowling's third Harry Potter adventure: THE PRISONER OF AZKABAN. This was a stunt, set up by a London bookshop, to attract as much attention as possible.

It worked, too. As part of a nationwide publicity campaign, the stunt helped generate more coverage from the press, radio and television than most children's authors can hope for in a whole career of writing.

That's unless Harry Potter was working some of his magic in real life, of course...

Who could blame him if he did? For books, even by authors with an impressive track record, are easily upstaged by more in-your-face ways of having fun. This is why publishers are delighted if there's a movie or TV adaptation of one of their titles. They call it a 'tie-in' – and exploit it like mad in order to sell as many copies as they can. Admittedly, the movie may be AWFUL. But whoever heard of a book with sales that went down after being transferred to the screen? Watch what happens to the Harry Potter series after Hollywood's finest have had their way with it!

OPRAH'S BOOK CLUB

Who says television is the arch-enemy of books? Each month, the Oprah Winfrey Show in America features a new book... there's usually a short film about how it came to be written followed by a discussion between four or five readers, Oprah herself and the author. The result? Twenty-eight bestsellers have been created since 1996 – with total sales of more than twenty million copies. Hmmm... how long before we have a programme like this here in Britain?

Most books aren't made into movies, though. So how can one particular title possibly hope to catch our eye? Publishers rely on their sales and marketing specialists to solve this problem.

The Sales Force

These are the men and women who visit bookshops, libraries and schools with examples from their publisher's 'list' – the front-list features new books and the back-list contains books which may have been in print for some time but are still available. Sales reps need to know their stock inside-out so as to persuade as many customers as they can that they have titles which mustn't be missed or need re-ordering immediately.

The Publicity Team

They are responsible for producing the publisher's catalogue – an up-to-date account of all the company's books still in print plus background and sales information. They organise other materials, too,

from posters and bookmarks to balloons and author profiles. If an important book is given a 'launch' party, they fix it. Most important of all, they keep in touch with journalists and critics – sending out free copies in the hope of a good review.

Of course, they may get the opposite. But with so many books being published, even a mention in the media is welcome. Authors know this only too well. Almost all of them are convinced their books would be bestsellers if only more was being done to 'push' their work. So they have to be treated... tactfully.

Publicity is always a bit of a balancing act. If it's too aggressive it may even provoke a backlash. For instance, one TV interviewer did her best to suggest that it wasn't the brilliance of the writing which made the Harry Potter books so popular. 'Aren't the real brains at Bloomsbury, the publishers?' she asked.

Imagine how J. K. Rowling felt about that.

Luckily for her, and other writers, there's another way of nudging books into the limelight.

Prizes and Awards

At one level these are just plain daft. What sense does it really make to say a collection of Kit Wright's poems is better, or worse, than a story by Adèle Geras or a science fiction novel by Douglas Hill? Each may be equally enjoyable, and equally excellent, on its own terms.

This doesn't stop us trying to pick the 'best', though.

OSCARS FOR AUTHORS

Britain has never had so many awards and prizes for children's books as exist today. Every aspect is covered from 'lifetime achievement' to 'most promising debut', from book covers to 'best combination of words and pictures', from Science texts to Special Needs.

For a full and detailed list – including the awards where children play a key part – consult THE CHILDREN'S BOOK HANDBOOK, published annually by Young Book Trust in London. This lists no less than twenty-eight different prizes nationwide, which are awarded over eleven months of each calendar year.

In August, of course, everyone's assumed to be on holiday.

Nowadays, there's an ever-increasing number of gongs and trophies authors can win. Writers for adults may dream of the Nobel Prize for Literature; for children's authors it's the Hans Christian Andersen Award. Whether it's the Booker, the Whitbread, the Carnegie Medal or the Smarties Prize – and these are just a few examples of British awards – you can bet that somewhere, right now, a judging panel is racking its brains about the books piled in front of it. However dodgy, book prizes are here to stay.

My guess is that they meet two very important human needs. One is our need to compare – to find some sort of pattern in our likes and dislikes so we don't feel overwhelmed by them. The other is our need to celebrate – to make a glorious ring-a-ding fuss about something we care about. When we pick out the amazing skill or vision of a particular book or writer, we're saying a loud hip-hip-hooray for the skill and vision of books and writers generally. Also, we're recognising that in the case of some books and some writers this skill and vision seems exceptional – like lightning that's especially bright or strikes over and over again in the same place.

Okay, so perhaps the judges get it wrong sometimes. Afterwards, they may be utterly baffled by the prize-winning choices they made. Or the ones they didn't make. At the time, though, that's how they felt. And at least they were brave enough to say so. So let's not be too hard on book awards – especially those which give ordinary readers a say as well as the so-called experts.

For it's the enthusiasm of ordinary readers which makes books matter in the end. And this includes the most important reader of this book.

Who's that? You! So forget that end-of-term report or your latest SAT result. We're talking real enthusiasm here. Remember what Adrian Mitchell said about his poems: 'I'm glad if people who like them read them aloud, sing them, dance them or act them in school. And even happier if they choose to learn any of them by heart.'

AUTHORS IN PERSON

Listening to authors reading from their work has always been a special treat for readers. In the 14th century, Geoffrey Chaucer read his poems to King Richard II and Queen Anne. Two centuries later, playgoers may have seen Shakespeare himself in performance. Three centuries after that, Charles Dickens became almost as famous for reading his work as writing it – audiences in Britain and America flocked to hear the great man in action.

Today, the tradition is still alive and well… nearly all writers and illustrators for children make regular Author Visits to schools and libraries. Have you met any of your favourites?

If books don't get enough reading aloud, singing, dancing, acting and learning by heart in your school, you really must do your duty.

In the nicest possible way, grumble.

Better still, help your teachers kick-start a change of direction by setting up a Book Week or Reading Festival with one of your favourite authors as the star guest. Children's Book Week (the second week in October) or World Book Day (the first Thursday of March) are probably best avoided, however, because that's when everyone wants a visitor. Your local library, or Schools' Library Service will give you advice on the details. So will The Book Trust in London or a specialist agency like Speaking of Books which organises visits by storytellers, illustrators and writers all over the country. Admittedly, most of them will charge a fee for their time. But so do supply-teachers and school inspectors.

Who will be the most fun, though?

And who might leave you with a book that's been signed for you personally?

A signed copy of my favourite book?

Maybe locking a book in a cage isn't such a weird idea after all…

10
FUTURE BOOKS

Imagine this conversation between a couple of keen, but very worried, book lovers:

This is a pretty depressing discussion. But isn't it roughly what we'd expect, give or take a few shifts in language, from a pair of monks in the 15th century when they realised their hand written books were being challenged by the invention of the new-fangled printing press?

Ahh... did you think they were a couple of today's die-hard bookworms worrying about the onslaught of e-books?

Well, they could have been. That's the trouble with technology... for those who hate change it's downright scary. Sometimes it's right to be scared, too. Only a century or so after the invention of the printing press, the monkish manuscript industry had all but collapsed. That's not the end of the story, though. Consider, for example, HORAE BEATAE MARIAE AD USUM ROMANUM...

It's Latin... the name of a famous Book of Hours. Compiled and illustrated in France in 1524, this one-off volume is one of the last great glories of the parchment age. In those days, life was a lot shorter and nastier than it is now, and this collection of psalms, prayers and extracts from the Bible was intended to remind the reader that only Holiness brings true happiness.

No one knows whose beautiful handwriting we're looking at here, though. And no one knows who was involved in the forty-two exquisitely coloured illustrations – so detailed that scholars reckon they must have been painted under a magnifying glass. The book is so old and delicate, that only scholars able to travel to the Library of Congress in America, can get a proper look at it.

Until now, that is.

In January 2000, HORAE BEATAE MARIAE AD USUM ROMANUM was produced as a CD-rom. It was so accurate that one reviewer claimed he could 'smell the parchment'. What he could also do was listen to a translation from the Latin, check out an expert commentary on how this sort of book was used and examine its pages more closely than anyone ever before – including whoever produced them. And all for the price of a hardback.

Hmmm... even our two whinging friars might be tempted to click on to a piece of inspired wizardry like this.

It should also inspire us with confidence. Of course the future's uncertain – it always is – but why should that mean everything has to be worse? That's seldom the case with technology for at least two reasons:

1. Technology doesn't dis-invent what's gone before. It tends to re-invent it in order to do the job better. The printed book was certainly bad news for the hand-made book... but how can we possibly claim it was bad for books generally? Why shouldn't the arrival of the electronic book boost reading in just the same way?

2. Technology isn't just for technologists. If it were, then printed books would have been read only by printers. In fact, William Caxton made sure his first typeface resembled handwritten letters – because that's what was expected by readers at that time.

Nowadays, readers have a much wider choice than in William Caxton's day. So an e-book needs to match, or even improve, what we love about the printed book. After all, reading that requires a full-size computer terminal is as limiting as reading that needs a full-size lectern. That's why the race is on to make e-books as simple, handy, reliable, long-lasting and neat as an ordinary, everyday paperback.

Plus a bit of extra singing-and-dancing, of course. For some kinds of reading – of stories and poems, say – this might not amount to much in the end. Technological trickery may even get in the way of our enjoyment. If this is the case, then we'd do better to stick with the medium that's already proved itself: books.

A LIBRARY IN THE PALM OF YOUR HAND

Rocket e-books are already with us. They weigh about twenty ounces, can download about ten book's worth of text from the internet and light up for reading in the dark.

Of course, they don't feel like a book, get rather heavy after a while and it's easy to lose your place as you scroll down the pages. That's now, though. Soon, the current format may look as antiquated as a gramophone record. As a what, do I hear you say? Precisely... now we call them CDs.

BOOK THEFT

Ancient books can be very valuable and a target for thieves. In the 1990s, a gang called The Astronomers stole a number of old scientific treatises from the university libraries of Eastern Europe which are often poorly guarded. As part of hauls worth more than £150 million, The Astronomers got away with Ptolomy's COSMOGRAPHIA, written in ancient Egypt, and Copernicus's CONCERNING THE REVOLUTIONS OF THE HEAVENLY BODIES, printed in 1543.

The worst book thief of all time, though, was probably an Italian, Count Libri (1803–1869). He spent a profitable lifetime plundering French libraries for rare and expensive tomes. When Libri was discovered, he was sacked from his job at the Institut de France. Some time later, his successor was persuaded to buy an autograph collection which included the signatures of Julius Caesar, Pythagoras, Nero, Cleopatra and Mary Magdalen. Eventually, these were all proved to be forgeries. Three guesses as to who was behind the scam!

For other kinds of reading, the opportunities for e-books look much more promising. Imagine how THE BOOK ABOUT BOOKS could be transformed:

- By back-up details on all the wonderful writers for children I've mentioned... along with a list, maybe in alphabetical order from Ashley to Zindel, of the equally wonderful writers I haven't found space for.

- By follow-up information on topics where I've been too brief, or maybe sparked off a particular reader's interest, more than I can hope to satisfy here.

- By animating Anderson... a chance for Scoular's sketches to steal the show even more!

- By a voice-over to help readers who can't cope with this pell-mell of pages.

- By...

But I'd better stop there.

With an e-book all the above is only a click away – a wealth of material that can support a text without swamping it.

As a book-lover, I'm beginning to feel faint again. So let me sign off with the question I asked ten chapters ago. Are books really so special that they deserve a book's worth of writing and drawing all to themselves?

YES!

If you've read this far, you probably agree with Scoular and me. In fact, we can't wait to get started on

our next one whether we're writing and illustrating it
ourselves, or just reading somebody else's.

Why don't you do the same?

USEFUL ADDRESSES

For general information:

Young Book Trust
Book House
45 East Hill
London
SW18 2QZ
Tel: 020 8516 2977
Fax: 020 8516 2978
Website:
www.booktrust.org.uk

The Library Association
7 Ridgmount Street
London
WC1E 7AE
Tel: 020 7436 7218
Website: www.la-hq.org.uk

Readathon
Swerford
Chipping Norton
Oxon
OX7 4BG
Tel/Fax: 01608 730335
Website: www.readathon.org

Scottish Book Trust
Scottish Book Centre
137 Dundee Street
Edinburgh
EH11 1BG
Tel: 0131 229 3663
Fax: 0131 228 4293
Website:
www.scottishbooktrust.com

For specialist information:

Reading and Language Information Centre
University of Reading
Bulmershe Court
Earley
Reading
RH40 4HT
Tel: 0118 931 8820
Fax: 0118 931 6801
Website:
www.ralic.rdg.ac.uk

REACH (National Resource Centre for Children with Reading Difficulties)
California Country Park
Nine Mile Road
Finchampstead
Berks
RG40 4HT
Tel: 0118 973 7575
Fax: 0118 973 7105
Helpline: 08445 604 0414
Website:
www.reach-reading.demon.co.uk

For Author Visits:

For 'do-it-yourself' contact:
The author's website if available, or his/her publisher

For specialist help contact:
Speaking of Books
9 Guildford Grove
Greenwich
London
SE10 8JY
Tel/Fax: 020 8692 4704
Email:
jan@speakingofbooks.co.uk
Websites:
www.speakingofbooks.co.uk
www.authorsinschools.co.uk

Three Helpful Publications

The Children's Book Handbook – 2000 Edition
ISBN 0-8535-3478-0
(contact Young Book Trust)

Making Books by Paul Johnson
Published by A & C Black
ISBN 0-7136-5077-X

Talking Books by James Carter
Published by Routledge
ISBN 0-4151-9417-2

Answers from p66:

Colin Hawkins – illustrator,
Jacqui Hawkins – writer

On the books they work on together, Laurence Anholt does the writing and Catherine does the illustrations. Laurence also illustrates his own books.

Janet Ahlberg – illustrator,
Allen Ahlberg – writer

BOOKS MENTIONED IN THE TEXT

Adamson, Jean and Gareth
Topsy and Tim series
Blackie, first published
1962

Ardley, Neil
The Way things Work
Dorling Kindersley, 1988
Eyewitness Guide to Music,
Dorling Kindersley, 1989
*101 Great Science
Experiments*
Dorling Kindersley, 1998

Blacker, Terence
The Transfer
Macmillan, 1998

Blake, Quentin
Mr Magnolia
Jonathan Cape, 1983
Clown
Joanthan Cape, 1995
Zagazoo
Jonathan Cape, 1998

Blume, Judy
Forever
Gollancz, 1976

Briggs, Raymond
Fungus the Bogeyman
Hamish Hamilton, 1977
The Snowman
Hamish Hamilton, 1978

Brisley, Joyce Lancaster
Milly-Molly-Mandy series
Harrap, first published
1928

Browne, Anthony
Piggybook
Julia MacRae, 1986

Burgess, Melvin
Junk
Andersen Press, 1996

Crompton, Richmal
Just William series
Macmillan, first published
1922

Cross, Gillian
The Great Elephant Chase
Puffin, 1994
The Demon Headmaster
Oxford University Press, 1996

Dahl, Roald
The BFG
Jonathan Cape, 1982

Fine, Anne
Madam Doubtfire
Hamish Hamilton, 1987

Grahame, Kenneth
The Wind in the Willows
Methuen, 1908

Hughes, Shirley
Dogger
Bodley Head, 1977

Hutchins, Pat
Rosie's Walk
Bodley Head, 1970

King-Smith, Dick
The Sheep-Pig
Gollancz, 1983
The Hodgeheg
Hamish Hamilton, 1987

Lindgren, Astrid
Pippi Longstocking
Penguin, 1976

Milne, A.A.
Winnie the Pooh
Methuen, 1926

Mitchell, Adrian
*Balloon Lagoon and the
Magic Islands of Poetry*
Orchard, 1997

Nesbit, E.
*The Story of the Treasure
Seekers*
Unwin, 1899

Nimmo, Jenny
The Snow Spider
Methuen, 1986

Pullman, Philip
His Dark Materials:
Scholastic
Northern Lights, 1995
The Subtle Knife, 1997
The Amber Spyglass, 2000

Ransome, Arthur
Swallows and Amazons
Jonathan Cape, first published 1930

Robinson, Joan G.
Teddy Robinson
Harrap, first published 1953

Rosen, Michael
Quick let's get out of here
Andre Deutsch, 1983

Rowling, J.K.
*Harry Potter and the
Prisoner of Azkaban*
Bloomsbury, 1999

Sendak, Maurice
Where the Wild Things Are
Bodley Head, 1967

Swindells, Robert
Brother in the Land
Oxford University Press, 1984

Waddell, Martin
The Park in the Dark
Walker, 1989

Wilson, Jacqueline
Double Act
Yearling, 1996
The Illustrated Mum
Doubleday, 1999